The Shakespeare Revue

First presented by the RSC as part of the Barbican Centre's International Shakespeare Festival in October 1994, *The Shakespeare Revue* gathers together some of the finest comic material inspired by Shakespeare. Incorporating many previously unpublished items, the revue ranges from the sharply satirical to the broadly comic, pausing occasionally to reflect more seriously on its theme. It is delightfully illustrated by leading theatre caricaturists, cartoonists and designers.

CHRISTOPHER LUSCOMBE began his career writing and performing for the Footlights Revue at Cambridge. He worked extensively in rep before appearing at the Old Vic in *Kean*, and then joined the Royal Shakespeare Company, with whom he has spent the last four years. His many roles have included Dapper in *The Al--*   *Artists and Admirers*, Moth in   Launcelot Gobbo in *The Mer-*   e-man show *Half Time,* co-   neville, has been seen at the   ar Warehouse and on tour.

played leading roles in theatres the country – Sir Benjamin Backbite in *The School for Scandal*, Mephistophiles in *Doctor Faustus*, Trinculo in *The Tempest* and the Dentist in *Little Shop of Horrors*. He has devised a number of revues – *The Cocktail Hour, End of Term, Theatrical Digs* – and composed scores for many plays and musicals in the theatre, including *A Midsummer Night's Dream, The Tempest* and *Torch Song Trilogy*. For radio his scores include *Tom and Viv, Time and the Conways, The Good Companions* and *The Schoolmistress*, and he is currently adapting *Oh, What a Lovely War!* to be heard on Radio 4 in 1995. He also works as a freelance graphic designer.

THE
𝕾hakespeare
REVUE

compiled by

CHRISTOPHER LUSCOMBE

and

MALCOLM MCKEE

with a foreword by

ADRIAN NOBLE

NICK HERN BOOKS

London

A Nick Hern Book

The Shakespeare Revue first published in Great Britain in 1994 as a paperback original by Nick Hern Books Limited, 14 Larden Road, London W3 7ST

Copyright in the compilation, introduction and editorial material © 1994 by Christopher Luscombe and Malcolm McKee

Copyright in the individual pieces and illustrations remains the property of the individual copyright owners: for details see Acknowledgements

Typeset by Country Setting, Woodchurch, Kent TN26 3TB

Printed in Great Britain by Cox and Wyman Ltd, Reading, Berks

A catalogue record for this book is available from the British Library

ISBN 1 85459 252 1

For
Carol, Kathy,
Sonja and Wayne

Contents

Illustrations

Foreword

I have always regarded comedy as a deeply serious art, and approached masters of the craft with considerable awe. They possess meticulous technique, cunningly disguised in a relaxed spontaneity; the results of their efforts are immediately and cruelly manifest – the audience either laugh or they don't. Small wonder then that the lunchtime hubub in the green room of the Bristol Old Vic when I started out as a director in the late seventies was always sharply divided: unrestrained hysteria and mirth from the actors rehearsing the tragedy and intense, urgent negotiations amongst those working on the comedy.

Christopher Luscombe and Malcolm McKee have compiled a revue, one of the trickiest and most elusive forms of comic entertainment. They have no storyline to support them; the art requires almost limitless gifts of characterisation, intellectual dexterity, versatility, lightness and delicacy of touch, precision. In other words, wit. The Elizabethans, of course, put a high price on wit – that ability to stimulate our intelligence while making us laugh – and regarded it as the natural accompaniment to all aspects of a civilised adult life.

Chris and Malcolm's *Shakespeare Revue* celebrates Shakespeare by showing us his reflection in the ink of dozens of authors and wits. Falstaff boasts 'I am not only witty in myself, but the cause that wit is in other men.' *The Shakespeare Revue* spectacularly applies the same maxim to Shakespeare and succeeds in full measure.

ADRIAN NOBLE
Artistic Director, RSC

Introduction

The idea for *The Shakespeare Revue* came about on Shakespeare's birthday, 23 April 1993, when the RSC was planning a celebratory service in Stratford's Holy Trinity Church. Light relief was needed among other more serious readings, and in searching for something suitable, we were reminded of just how many comic writers have used Shakespeare as raw material for their work. Unearthing such pieces became a hobby, until eventually the outline of a stage show began to emerge. We had no thought of publication until it became evident that – amazingly in the Shakespeare Industry – nobody seemed to have got there before us.

Of course, there's far too much material for one volume, so we gave ourselves certain restrictions. We resisted the somewhat academic connotations of the conventional anthology, opting instead for genuinely theatrical revue material – much of it no longer readily available.

So the backbone of this collection is a range of work which represents the development of revue itself – from Music Hall to Victoria Wood, via Farjeon, Melville, Footlights and the Fringe. We hope the other extracts from musicals, radio broadcasts, comic novels and the like, fit into a coherent whole, and we've tried to juxtapose them in such a way as to make linking passages superfluous. In keeping with the spirit of revue, we have included some straight material, to lend the programme an element of light and shade.

Of all literary and theatrical forms, revue is one of the least documented. With no authoritative reference book to guide us, our quest for material took us from the manuscript collection of the British Library to a home for retired variety performers in Twickenham, via June Whitfield's attic. We must have overlooked many gems along the way, and we have deliberately omitted one or two famous names, preferring to include a proportion of lesser-known work.

Every aspect of this project – research, performance and publication – has been eased by the help we have received from a long list of individuals to whom we are extremely grateful. We apologise in advance to anyone whom we miss out. First and foremost, we are conscious of the generosity of all the authors and illustrators. A full list of acknowledgements appears on page 104.

We have been given encouragement and practical assistance by many members of the RSC, particularly Adrian Noble (to whom we are also indebted for his delightful Foreword), David Brierley, Jonathan Pope, Stephen Browning, Graham Sawyer, Zoë Mylchreest, Charles Evans, Sally Barling, Clare Burgess, Anne Tippett, Alex Bannock and Amanda Hunt. The original script was typed by Sheonagh Darby, proof-read by Richard Bonneville, Rex Bunnett, Kathy Elgin and Frank Middlemass, and seen through typesetting by Simon Trussler. We've also been grateful for the enthusiasm of the Friends of the RSC, led by Maire Steadman, Jean Williams and Leslie Berry.

Then there are those who went out of their way to help us find particular pieces: Donald Anderson, Ronnie Barker, Raymond Bowers, Bille Brown, Rex Bunnett, Alan Coren, Barry Cryer, Jonathan Cullen, John Dankworth, Lyn Darnley, David Delve, Gordon Dickerson, Gervase Farjeon, Michael Frayn, Bamber

Gascoigne, Benny Green, Wendy Greenhill, Lyn Haill, Anne Harvey, Nigel Hess, Roy Hudd, Ian Hughes, Debbie Humphreys, Barry Humphries, Clive James, Mary-Jane Jeanes, Ian Judge, Dillie Keane, David King, Michael Kustow, Audrey Lane, Cleo Laine, Patricia Lancaster, David Lodge, Kitty and Catherine Maceluch, John Moffatt, Sheridan Morley, Jon Naismith, Jean Perkins, Martin Phillips, Patsy Pollock, Harry Porter, Roger Pringle, Carol Redford, Elliott Reid, Griff Rhys Jones, Amanda Root, Jeremy Sams, Robert Smallwood, David Swift, Barry Took, Andrew Wade, Allan Watkins, Edward Watson, James Wellman, John Wells, Stanley Wells, David Weston, June Whitfield, Aubrey Woods, Guy and Jane Woolfenden, Anita Wright, Geoffrey Wright, Shirley and Alan Wright, Stephen Wyatt, Gary Yershon, British Actors' Equity Association, the British Music Hall Society, the Cartoon Gallery, the Performing Right Society, the Shakespeare Centre and The Spotlight.

The other members of the original cast – David Delve, Debra Gillett and Abigail McKern – gave up precious free time to try out our various draft scripts; their commitment and expertise were invaluable in shaping the final version. We are also most grateful to Rob Howell, our designer, and Chris de Wilde, our production manager. We have been patiently guided through the unfamiliar world of book production by our agent Alan Brodie and our publisher Nick Hern. Finally, a special mention for the resourceful RSC quartet of Sonja Dosanjh (Company Manager), Wayne Dowdeswell (Lighting Designer), Kathy Elgin (Head of Publications) and Carol Malcolmson (Head of Planning), without whom we would never have reached the point of writing this Introduction. To all, our sincere thanks.

CHRISTOPHER LUSCOMBE AND MALCOLM MCKEE
Barbican Theatre, August 1994

The Shakespeare Revue

was first performed by the Royal Shakespeare Company in The Pit on 30 October 1994 as part of the Barbican Centre's *Everybody's Shakespeare* Festival, in a performance sponsored by Allied Domecq. The cast comprised David Delve, Debra Gillett, Christopher Luscombe, Malcolm McKee and Abigail McKern. The production was directed by Christopher Luscombe and Malcolm McKee and designed by Rob Howell, with lighting by Wayne Dowdeswell. A shortened version was recorded by BBC Radio for transmission at Christmas. The producer was Sue Wilson.

Note

Almost every item in *The Shakespeare Revue* has been subjected to a number of minor cuts and, very occasionally, to rewrites. This has been necessary to achieve a flow from one piece to the next, and to allow some longer extracts to fit into a revue format. For details of how to find the uncut versions, please see the acknowledgements on page 104.

Part One

Prologue

Robert Graves said that 'the remarkable thing about Shakespeare is that he is really very good – in spite of all the people who say he's very good.'

Bernard Shaw said: 'There is no eminent writer I despise so entirely as I despise Shakespeare when I measure my mind against his.'

And Tolstoy wrote to Chekhov: 'Shakespeare's plays are bad enough, but yours are even worse.'

J.M.Barrie said: 'I know not whether Bacon wrote the works of Shakespeare, but if he did not it seems to me he missed the opportunity of his life.'

Charlie Chaplin said: 'I am not concerned with who wrote the works of Shakespeare, but I hardly think it was the Stratford boy.'

And Henry James said: 'The divine William is the most successful fraud ever practised on a patient world.'

Shakespeare was a dramatist of note;
He lived by writing things to quote.

Quoting Shakespeare

If you cannot understand my argument, and declare 'It's Greek to me', you are quoting Shakespeare.

If you claim to be more sinned against than sinning, you are quoting Shakespeare.

If you recall your salad days, you are quoting Shakespeare.

If you act more in sorrow than anger, if your wish is father to the thought, if your lost property has vanished into thin air, you are quoting Shakespeare.

If you have ever refused to budge an inch, or suffered from green-eyed jealousy, if you have played fast and loose, if you have been tongue-tied, a tower of strength, hoodwinked or in a pickle, if you have knitted your brows, made a virtue of necessity, insisted on fair play or slept not one wink, had short shrift, cold comfort or too much of a good thing, if you have seen better days or lived in a fool's paradise – why, be that as it may, the more fool you, for it's a foregone conclusion that you are (as good luck would have it) quoting Shakespeare.

If you think it is early days and clear out bag and baggage, if you think it is high time and that that is the long and short of it, if you believe that the game is up and that truth will out even if it involves your own flesh and blood, then – to give the devil his due – if the truth were known (for surely you have a tongue in your head) you are quoting Shakespeare.

Even if you bid me good riddance and send me packing, if you wish I were dead as a doornail, if you think I am an eyesore, a laughing stock, the devil incarnate, a stony-hearted villain, bloody-minded or a blinking idiot, then – by Jove!

O Lord!

Tut, tut!

For goodness' sake!

What the dickens!

But me no buts!

It's all one to me,

For you are quoting Shakespeare.

Bernard Levin
From *Enthusiasms* (1983)

Song: *Brush Up Your Shakespeare*

The girls today in society go for classical poetry,
So to win their hearts one must quote with ease
Aeschylus and Euripides.
But the poet of them all, who will start them simply ravin',
Is the poet people call 'The Bard of Stratford-on-Avon'.

Cole Porter
From the musical *Kiss Me Kate* (1948)

Who was William Shakespeare?

And so it was, at the dawning of the Elizabethan Epoch, as it was known – that a babe was born in a small well-known English Midlands town called Stratford-upon-Avon (or Stratford East, Stratford Ontario or Stratford Johns, as it was also known) – home of Anne Hathaway's Cottage, Mary Arden's House, Shakespeare's Birthplace and the Royal Shakespeare Theatre Company.

And as his parents gazed down at that little new-born Elizabethan infant, his little Elizabethan ruff already round his little rough Elizabethan neck, his little struggling Elizabethan body already clad in his first little all-in-one doublet and hose, and proudly watched him mewling and puking all over his brand new little

Elizabethan duvet, they could not possibly have guessed what that recently sired babe – fruit of their handiwork, so to speak – *would in fact become.*

For the babe that lay before them – and already showing signs, *even as an infant*, of his famous prematurely receding forehead – was none other than that Son of Avon, the Immortal Swan himself, William Shakespeare.

In other words, the most famous man the world has ever known.

But who in fact was he?

Will we ever find out?

Or will he always remain 'shrouded in mystery'?

To answer these questions, and many more, we must now consider 'Who was William Shakespeare'?

William Geoffrey Shakespeare was born in Shakespeare's Birthplace in Stratford-upon-Avon but a stone's throw from Anne Hathaway's Cottage with whom he was to have a stormy and incestuous marriage in later years.

Unfortunately, this is all that is currently known of the extraordinary and colourful life of William Shakespeare. Which leads us, of course, to the question: *Who was William Shakespeare?*

In order to answer this we need first to ask ourselves two further questions:

1. Who were his parents?

Although – as we have seen – nothing whatsoever is known about his parents, we *do* know, via combing through various records and so forth, that his father was George Shakespeare or possibly even Thomas Shakespeare, a well-known Elizabethan glove maker from Stratford's Glove Quarter (or 'Compartment', as it was also known), while his mother, of course, was Mary Arden, the popular Stratford cosmetics expert.

2. Did he get on with his parents, generally?

Yes, he certainly did. In fact, they never had any rows or suchlike, fortunately.

3. Did Shakespeare's father's glove manufacturing influence Shakespeare's early works?

Yes, it certainly did. Shakespeare's early works are stiff with glove-manufacturing references. In fact, many whole plays were inspired by his father's obsession with constantly inventing new kinds of glove. In particular, the woollen glove which inspired *The Winter's Tale,* the animal-handling glove which inspired *The Taming of the Shrew* and, of course, the rubber glove which inspired *Pericles – Prince of Tyre.*

Patrick Barlow
From *Shakespeare: the Truth* (1993)

9

The Music Hall Shakespeare

Shakespeare wrote a lot of plays,
Tragedies of olden days –
Wrote 'em in a manner far from gay.
Often it occurs to me
How much brighter they would be
Written in a 'music hally' way.
Take 'To be or not to be',
Hamlet's famed soliloquy –
Nowadays the point it seems to miss;
But revise the words a bit,
Put a catchy tune to it,
And Hamlet's speech would turn out
   more like this:

CHORUS
(to the tune of *Let's all go down the Strand*)

To be, or not to be?
To be, or not to be?
If I live, Ophelia I must wed;
If I die, I'll be a long time dead.
To be, or not to be? (That is the question.)
I'm fairly up a tree.
If I die, where shall I go?
Even John Bull doesn't know.
To be, or not to be.

Take another Shakespeare play,
Very gruesome I must say,
In which Shylock plays a leading part.
He's the chap, I'm sure you know,
Who from young Antonio
Claims a pound of flesh cut near the heart.
Anger flashing from his eyes,
'Curse the Christian dog' he cries,
'I will have my pound of flesh this day.'
How much nicer it would be

If, instead of tragedy,
Shylock to Antonio did say:

CHORUS
(to the tune of *Oh! Oh! Antonio*)

'Oh! Oh! Antonio! You'll have to pay.
Though you are stoney-o
I'll get my own-y-o.
I'll have my pound of flesh
Cut from your heart,
And I'll hawk it round at fourpence a pound
On my ice-cream cart.'

Next a character I'll quote,
From a play that Shakespeare wrote –
King Henry VIII – a wicked lot!
Half a dozen wives had he,
'Cos when with one he couldn't agree,
He divorced her, and a fresh one got.
Till at last, in righteous wrath,
Wolsey cried out 'By my troth,
This man's a libertine – off with his head!'
But if that had been a play
On the music halls today,
Wolsey would have simply winked and said:

CHORUS
(to the tune of *It's a Different Girl Again*)

'Hello! Hello! Hello! It's a different wife again;
With different eyes, different nose,
Different hair, different clothes.
Hello! Hello! Hello! To me it's fairly plain
He's tickled the chin of Anne Boleyn,
It's a different wife again.'

Words by **Worton David**
Music by **Harry Fragson** (*c.* 1905)

12

Othello

Now then, this geyser Othello was a moor – no
relation to the Old Moore wot wrote the Almanac,
nor to that well-known character Mrs Moore,
wot was told by 'er doctor not to 'ave any more,
Mrs Moore.

This Othello was great friends wiv a bloke called
Brabantio, a rich J.P. wot made 'is money sellin'
second-hand blinds to the Venetians, and 'e 'ad a
smashin' daughter called Desdemona, for whose 'and
and 'eart there was a bit of a queue.

Now this Desdemona was a funny wench, inasmuch
as she wanted a lover wot 'ad got somethin' wot the
others 'adn't got, wiv the result that when Othello
said 'Wot about it?' she didn't even say 'Wot about
wot?' – she knew, so they got quietly 'itched up.

When 'er old man found out wot she 'ad bin and
gone and done, 'e 'ad Othello nicked, for, as
Brabantio said, 'By spells and witchcraft' 'e 'ad
seduced the affections of 'is daughter without 'is
consent, which, boiled down, meant 'e'd 'ad a bash
without askin'.

Now then, when Othello came up for trial, the Judge
sez, 'Wot shall I do wiv 'im?' and Brabantio sez,
'Well, to start wiv, I propose we castigate 'im.' The
Judge sez, 'Maybe it's a little late now, still it's an
idea.' 'Owever Othello was saved from 'aving 'is
prospects for life ruined, 'cos at that moment the
VBBC (that was the Venetian Blind Broadcasting

Corporation) gave out as 'ow there was an invasion, so the War Office pulled some red tape and got Othello out on bail.

Othello is now in a bit of a mess. The Government wants 'im to finish orf the Invaders, and Desdemona wants 'im to finish orf the honeymoon. In 'is dilemma, 'e sez, 'Oh that I could cut myself in 'arf,' and Desdemona coyly sez, 'It's OK wiv me as long as I get the right 'arf.'

Leon Cortez (1946)

"LOOK TO YOUR WIFE; OBSERVE HER WELL WITH CASSIO." (OTHELLO)

Song: **Who is Silvia?**

Who is Silvia, what is she,
That all our swains commend her?
Holy, fair and wise is she;
The heaven such grace did lend her,
That admired she might be,
That admired she might be.

Then to Silvia let us sing,
That Silvia is excelling;
She excels each mortal thing
Upon the dull earth dwelling.
Let us garlands to her bring,
Let us garlands to her bring.

Words by **William Shakespeare**
Music by **Franz Schubert** (1826)

I'm in the RSC!

April 1977:
I'm in the RSC!
I'm in the RSC!
This is the right place, the best place for me!
To look out at that audience, to stand here on this
    stage!
Possibly-the-greatest-Shakespearean-actor-perhaps-of-
    my-age!
O! I could do this kind of work forever and
    forever!
And I'll say that the moment I get to meet
    Trevor.

I'm in the RSC!
I'm *in* the RSC!
I'm in *the* RSC!
I'm in the R*S*C!
I'm in the RSC!
And it's just amazing that *they* pay *me*!
I've got a tiny part in
The thing with John Barton;
I'm just a fairy
For Terry,
But then I am just startin'.
The main thing is hard work and keenness and
    endeavour.
I'm bound to be noticed before long by Trevor.

But O! For shame! *Disillusioned* I feel!
Now starts my head from confusion to reel.
Methinks I consented, aye, foolishly fast,
Signing a contract to play just 'as cast'.

I stand mute on battlements, mounds, rocks
    and carts,
Now understudy I seventeen parts.
Henceforth to have my voice heard I'll persever;
I'll SSSSENNND FOR A PARLEYYYYY!!!
I wanna see Trevor.

I've been covered in mud, I've shrieked up the aisle
For Bogdanov and Davies and Daniels and Kyle;
I've faffed with Francesca, ha-ha-ha'd around Helen,
Been gobbed on by Pennington, Sinden, McKellen.
I sit outside Trev's office from dawn till eleven
While he trevs Melvyn Bragg and he trevs
    André Previn;
Six months later, and he's still yammerin'.
(Nothing stops meetings with Andrew and Cameron.)

ROMEO & JULIET
MARIE KEAN as Nurse
FRANCESCA ANNIS as Juliet
IAN McKELLEN as Romeo
MICHAEL PENNINGTON as Mercutio

I'm tired of being A Roman, A Trojan, A Greek;
Tired of yelping and moaning – I JUST WANT TO
SPEAK!
I watch them cock it up through scenes everlasting –
I just don't understand their ideas about casting.
How could that gnome
Be the noblest in Rome?
Why has that pisser
Been given Nerissa?
I've heard that Joe Melia's
Been offered Cordelia!

Nightly crippling my body and gunging my face,
Whooh! things'd be different if I ran this place.
We're WORLD FOCUS, don't you see, so it's bound
to be tough;
We're good – yes, of course we're good –
But, come on, are we GOOD ENOUGH?
And OK, so SUDDENLY they're offering me Prince
Hal, Hamlet, Volumnia and Richard Three –
Well, too bad, they can stick it, they've done
NOTHING for me.
And I'll bring all this up if I get to see EVER
That elusive, fffly-by-night, absentee – TREVOR!!!
How ARE you? They all say that *Cats* is brilliantly
clever . . .

Jack Klaff (1981)

18

Song: **Witches' Brew**

(*Spoken*)
When shall we three meet again?
In thunder, lightning, or in rain?

(*Sung*)
When? When? When shall we three meet again?
Double, double, toil and trouble;
Fire burn, and cauldron bubble.
Eye of newt, and toe of frog,
And wool of bat, and tongue of dog,
And adder's fork, and blind-worm's sting,
And lizard's leg and howlet's wing.
And double, double, toil and trouble;
Fire burn and cauldron bubble tonight . . .

Words by **William Shakespeare,
Betty Comden** and **Adolph Green**
Music by **Jule Styne**
From the musical *Hallelujah, Baby!* (1967)

'More newts – Macbeth is staying to dinner.'

Song: *Which Witch?*

It is many a year since I launched my career in
Shakespeare.
At a most tender age I first tottered on stage as a
page.
If you happened to see Mistress Quickly with Tree,
that was me.
Coming right up to date, with Frank Benson the late
I played Kate.

Ah, those were the days, I'm sure you'll agree,
But last week a young chap from the famed RSC
(I think he's called Noble, I'm not really sure)
Rang me up and invited me out on a tour
For eighty-nine weeks as a witch in *Macbeth* –
A prospect I thought little better than death.
But as I'd grown tired of just giving auditions,
I said I would do it on certain conditions.

I said 'Mr Noble, Adrian dear,
There is one point on which I'm not clear.
We've fixed up the sordid finance, so to speak,
And I'm working for practically nothing a week,
But in which part am I to appear?

'Which witch?
Is it first witch or second or which?
Don't think I insist on a part that is huge,
But I've never in sixty-nine years been a stooge.
The part must be one in which I'll get my teeth,
Not the witch who keeps shouting 'All Hail' on the
heath.
If it's the first witch, well then I should love it,

But if it's the second you know where you can
    shove it.
The tall scraggy thin one does not interest me;
I must be the hag with the gag in Act Three.
To avoid any last minute hitch,
Would you kindly inform me which witch?

'Yes, before I pack one single bag,
I must know in advance, dear, which hag.
When we're grouped round the cauldron and
    watching it bubble,
I must be well lit or else there'll be trouble.
We can fix up these things when we start to
    rehearse,
But I must be the harpy who's got the best curse.
I must say it's rather a joke
To offer this pig in a poke.
I've laughed 'til I've got quite a stitch.
Now I just want to know, dear, you old so-and-so,
    dear, which witch?'

When I'd done Mr Noble said 'Blast!
I will not have that bitch in the cast.'
It appeared that I'd quite queered my pitch,
So I never discovered which witch.

Words by **Alan Melville**
Music by **Charles Zwar**
From the revue *Sky High* (1942)

Actors Prepare

The actors are come hither. Over weeks
Rehearsals root and texts unfold their tales,
Until the town begins to witness signs
That tell the opening night is close at hand.
The entrance to the stage is cluttered up
With curious chunks of castle walls and thrones;
And tucked away in whirring attic rooms
The Wardrobe ladies burn the midnight oil;
Pallid directors hurry through the streets;
And in The Dirty Duck young actors sit
Word-perfect with their twenty lines, and pray
This meagre lot will not be cut to ten;
They never know the troubles of the star,
Watching the river from his dressing room,
Who can't remember lines and wonders how
He'll ever triumph on that daunting stage.

Roger Pringle
From *Portrait of a Stratford Year* (1985)

Shakespeare Masterclass

DIRECTOR: All right, let's start at the beginning shall we?

ACTOR: Right, yeh.

DIRECTOR: What's the word, what's the word, I wonder, that Shakespeare decides to begin his sentence with here?

ACTOR: Er, 'Time' is the first word.

DIRECTOR: Time, Time.

ACTOR: Yep.

DIRECTOR: And how does Shakespeare decide to spell it, Hugh?

ACTOR: T-I-M-E.

DIRECTOR: T-I?

ACTOR: M.

DIRECTOR: M-E.

ACTOR: Yep.

DIRECTOR: And what sort of spelling of the word is that?

ACTOR: Well it's the ordinary spelling.

DIRECTOR: It's the *ordinary* spelling, isn't it? It's the *conventional* spelling. So why out of all the spellings he could have chosen, did Shakespeare choose that one, do you think?

ACTOR: Well, um, because it gives us time in an ordinary sense.

DIRECTOR: Exactly, well done, good boy. Because it gives us time in an ordinary, conventional sense.

ACTOR: Oh, right.

DIRECTOR: So, Shakespeare has given us time in a conventional sense. But he's given us something else, Hugh. Have a look at the typography. What do you spy?

ACTOR: Oh, it's got a capital T.

DIRECTOR: Shakespeare's T is very much upper case, there, Hugh, isn't it? Why?

ACTOR: 'Cos it's the first word in the sentence.

DIRECTOR: Well I think that's *partly* it. But I think there's another reason too. Shakespeare has given us time in a *conventional* sense – and time in an *abstract* sense.

ACTOR: Right, yes.

DIRECTOR: All right? Think your voice can convey that, Hugh?

ACTOR: I hope so.

DIRECTOR: I hope so too. All right. Give it a go.

ACTOR: Just the one word?

DIRECTOR: Just the one word for the moment.

ACTOR: Yep. (*He howls the word*) TIME!

DIRECTOR: Wo, wo, wo. Where do we gather from?

ACTOR: Oh, the buttocks.

DIRECTOR: Always the buttocks. Gather from the buttocks. Thank you.

ACTOR: (*gathering*) Time!

DIRECTOR: Well, there are a number of things I liked about that, Hugh, there was . . . there was . . . there was a number of things I liked about that. All right, try it again, and this time try and bring in a sense of Troy falling, a sense of ruin, of folly, of anger, of decay, of hopelessness and despair, a sense of greed –

ACTOR: Ambition?

DIRECTOR: No, leave ambition out for the moment if you would, Hugh, of greed, of mortality, and of transience. All right? And try to suffuse the whole thing with a red colour . . .

ACTOR: Time!

DIRECTOR: What went wrong there, Hugh?

ACTOR: I don't know. I got a bit lost in the middle actually.

Stephen Fry and **Hugh Laurie**
From the revue *The Cellar Tapes* (1981)

The Coarse Actor

What is a Coarse Actor? An actor who can remember his lines, but not the order in which they come. An actor who performs in Church Halls. Often the scenery will fall down. Sometimes the Church Hall may fall down. Invariably his tights will fall down. He will usually be playing three parts – Messenger, 2nd Clown, an Attendant Lord. His aim is to upstage the rest of the cast. His hope is to be dead by Act II so that he can spend the rest of the evening in the pub. It is as the Shakespearean Clown, or, more often, assistant clown, that the Coarse Actor comes into his own:

Music flourish

'Tis Pity She's the Merry Wife of Henry VI (Part One)

Act One
Scene One
A room in the castle of St. Albans. Flourish. Enter hautboys. Enter King with Darlington, Doncaster, Retford, Grantham, Newark, Peterborough, Welwyn, Hitchin and their trains. Enter Coarse Actor carrying flagon of wine. Exeunt.

Music flourish
Scene Two
A woodland glade. Enter First Clown and Coarse Actor as Second Clown.

FIRST CLOWN: Mass, 'twould make a neat's tongue turn French tailor, and cry old sowter from here to Blackfriars, would it not?

SECOND CLOWN: Aye, marry and amen.

FIRST CLOWN: Tell me, neighbour Clodpony, why is a codpiece like a candle-maker?

SECOND CLOWN: Nay, I know not.

FIRST CLOWN: Mass, thou makest light of the jest; and in making light thou art a very candle-maker indeed. Ergo, thou art a codpiece.

SECOND CLOWN: Marry.

FIRST CLOWN: Prithee tell me, what thinkest thou of the king?

SECOND CLOWN: He is a worthy man.

FIRST CLOWN: Aye, 'twere a royal remark. 'Twould out from you to me and back again 'twere not so.

SECOND CLOWN: No more, I prithee, else I split my ribs with merriment.

FIRST CLOWN: Tell me, what is it that hath a horn and hath not a horn?

SECOND CLOWN: God's sonties, but I know not.

FIRST CLOWN: Why, a cuckold when Michaelmas falls on a Thursday.

SECOND CLOWN: But why at Michaelmas?

FIRST CLOWN: Mass, I cannot tell.

SECOND CLOWN: I am dumb at thy wit.

FIRST CLOWN: But let's away. We must to St. Albans to see the King.

Both exit, gibbering and mowing. There is the sound of people leaving the audience.

Michael Green
From *The Art of Coarse Acting* (1964)

Swap a Jest

FIRST CLOWN: Shall I tell thee a topical tale? Her
Majesty the Queen . . .

SECOND CLOWN: God bless her, God bless her.

FIRST CLOWN: . . . was descending from a coach the
other day into a puddle.

SECOND CLOWN: Into a puddle right up to her . . . ? – No.

FIRST CLOWN: No. And she said to Sir Walter Raleigh . . .

SECOND CLOWN: What did she say, what did she say?

FIRST CLOWN: Where are the cloaks?

SECOND CLOWN: And he replied . . .

FIRST CLOWN: First right and follow the rush matting.

SECOND CLOWN: I don't wish to know that – kindly
leave the Globe! Minstrel, prithee . . .

BOTH: *(sing)*

When the wheel of fortune runs you down,
And the heavens above are grey,
Just step a measure,
Swap a jest
And sing a roundelay.

Remember all the world's a stage,
That's what the poets say.
So step a measure,
Swap a jest
And sing a roundelay. (Hey nonny!)
Sing a roundelay. (It swingeth!)
Sing a roundelay!

Tim Brooke-Taylor and **Bill Oddie**
From the revue *Cambridge Circus* (1963)

Look Behind You, Hamlet!

We hear a few bars of the Take It From Here *theme.*

DAVID: And now, from 1954, we bring you *Take It From Here*, featuring the Keynotes with the BBC Revue Orchestra conducted by Harry Rabinowitz.

A recent periodical pointed out that the popularity of pantomimes is declining while the popularity of Shakespeare is rising. Surely, then, the obvious solution is to make a pantomime out of a Shakespearean play. For example, *Hamlet*.

DICK: Well, we're halfway through the second act and the scene is the Battlements at Elsinore. The applause you've just heard is for Rosencrantz and Guildenstern at the two pianos. They've taken their bow and the scene has changed to Elsinore Castle kitchen. In strides Hamlet, a swaggering figure in black tights.

JUNE: Oh, what a rogue and peasant slave am I, I'll help my mother bake an apple pie.

DICK: Hamlet puts down the sequin skull he's carrying and looks all round the stage.

JUNE: Now, don't forget all you children in the audience, if you see the Ghost, all shout out 'Look behind you, Hamlet!' And the little boy and girl who shout the loudest will get a Hopalong Polonius badge!

ALL: Look behind you, Hamlet!

DICK: *(laughs)* This is very amusing. The Ghost has just popped out of the pantry on a unicycle and disappeared into the larder. Now Hamlet calls his mother, Queen Gertrude.

JUNE: Mothah! Mothah!

JIM: (*as Dame*) Here we are, here we are, all girls together, Queen Gertrude herself – 'They call me Dirty Gertie 'cos me jokes are Danish Blue.' Oh girls, what a day I've had! What with that wicked Claudius pouring half a pint of 'ot lead down my old man's lughole – well, I ask you! I've hardly had time to rinse out my soliloquies. Now, where's that lad of mine? Hamlet, where *are* you!

JUNE: I'm here, mother. Oh, mother dear, I'm in love again. And this time I know it's going to be a success.

JIM: A success! I'd say it's more likely to be Ophelia ! (*Laughs*) Ophelia! Oh girls, I knew something was rotten in the State of Denmark.

JUNE: Ophelia! Yet do I love thee though o'ercast –

(*sings*) Does your mother know you're out, Ophelia,
Does she know that I would like to steal ya . . .

DICK: Hamlet and the Queen go into a soft shoe shuffle – when suddenly the door opens and in staggers Ophelia herself, soaked to the skin and carrying a bunch of Rosemary.

ALMA: Turn again Hamlet, Prince of Denmark!

JIM: Angels and Ministers of Grace defend us! Ophelia! Soaking wet and on her benders! What happenethèd?

ALMA: Thou knows't the willow which grows askant a stream?

JIM: I wot it well.

ALMA: I tripped over it.

JIM: You mean you've been – ?

ALMA: Yes, I've been – altogether – everybody!

ALL: (*sing*) Floating down the river on a Sunday afternoon . . .

DAVID: In that edition of *Take It From Here*, the part of Hamlet was played by June Whitfield, Gertrude by Jimmy Edwards and Ophelia by Alma Cogan.

Frank Muir and **Denis Norden**
From *Take It From Here* (1954)

Joe and Me at the Play

I went to the theatre Tuesday night, and did enjoy it
so,
Really had the most wonderful time, I went with me
cousin Joe.
My aunt came with us as chaperon, but she's as deaf
as a post.
We went to see that Shakespeare thing about an old
king's ghost.
Can't remember the name of the play, but I know it
was terribly sad,
With a handsome young feller all in black, who
pretended he'd gone mad.
He looked so weary and wretched, I don't wonder,
with such a part.
Fancy having to learn all that and saying it all by
heart!
The King was dressed in a satin suit and a lovely
train, all red,
And the Queen was the wife of the King and also the
wife of the ghost who was dead.
And there was a girl in a white silk dress, with
masses of golden hair,
I think she was sweet on the poor young man, but
he didn't seem to care.
He carried on like a perfect brute, and went away in
a rage,
Though he did come back for a kiss, and then, the
next time she came on stage,
She was carrying some lovely flowers and singing a
queer old song,
And I said to Joe, you mark my words, she won't be
with us long.

And sure enough, from something the Queen said to
the King, I found
The poor thing was fetching more flowers when she
went and got herself drowned.
They buried her, but in them days they didn't know
how to behave:
The young men started fighting and jumping right
into the grave.
When I am dead and laid in my grave, I do hope Joe
won't jump,
He's six foot two, weighs thirteen stone, he'd come
down an awful bump.
It wasn't really a cheerful play, there was too much
sobbing and sighing,
Cursing and killing and praying out loud, and a
horrible lot of dying.
Well, there was the ghost, to begin with, and then in
another scene
The young man killed an old man who was hidden
behind a screen.
The pretty girl got drowned, like I said, and the two
young men they fought
Right in front of the King and Queen and the whole
of the Royal Court.
The Queen died out at the back; the end was a
perfect riddle.
One died here and one died there, and the nice man
died in the middle.
Oh, it really was the most killing piece; but the nicest
part to us
Was walking home in the moonlight (Auntie went
home on the bus).
And Joe was so awfully clever; he quoted out of the
play:
'To be or not to be?' and it's to be – next May!

Anon (*c*. 1890)

33

Giving Notes

Right. Bit of hush please. Connie! Thank you. Now
that was quite a good rehearsal; I was quite pleased.
There were a few raised eyebrows when we let it
slip the Piecrust Players were having a bash at
Shakespeare but I think we're getting there. But I
can't say this too often: it may be *Hamlet* but it's got
to be Fun Fun Fun!

Now we're still very loose on lines. Where's Gertrude?
I'm not so worried about you – if you 'dry' just give
us a bit of business with the shower cap. But Barbara
– you will have to buckle down. I mean, Ophelia's
mad scene, 'There's rosemary, that's for remem-
brance' – it's no good just bunging a few herbs about
and saying, 'Don't mind me, I'm a loony'. Yes?

Right, Act One Scene One, on the ramparts. Now I
know the whist table is a bit wobbly, but until Stan
works out how to adapt the Beanstalk it'll have to
do. What's this? Atmosphere? Yes – now what did
we work on, Philip? Yes, it's midnight, it's jolly cold.
What do we do when it's cold? We go 'Brrr', and we
do this *(slaps hands on arms)*. Right, well don't forget
again, please. And cut the hot-water bottle, it's not
working.

Where's my ghost of Hamlet's father? Oh yes, what
went wrong tonight, Betty? He's on nights still, is he?
OK. Well, it's not really on for you to play that
particular part, Betty – you're already doing the
Player Queen and the back legs of Hamlet's donkey.
Well, we don't know he didn't have one, do we?
Why waste a good cossy?

Hamlet – drop the Geordie, David, it's not coming over. Your characterisation's reasonably good, David, but it's just far too gloomy. Fair enough, make him a little bit depressed at the beginning, but start lightening it from Scene Two, say from the hokey-cokey onwards.

Polonius, try and show the age of the man in your voice and in your bearing, rather than waving the bus-pass. I think you'll find it easier when we get the walking frame. Is that coming, Connie? OK.

The Players' scene: did any of you feel it had stretched a bit too . . . ? Yes. I think we'll go back to the tumbling on the entrance, rather than the extract from *Barnum*. You see, we're running at six hours twenty now, and if we're going to put those soliloquies back in . . .

Gravediggers? Oh yes, gravediggers. The problem here is that Shakespeare hasn't given us a lot to play with – I feel we're a little short on laughs, so Harold, you do your dribbling, and Arthur, just put in anything you can remember from the Ayckbourn, yes?

The mad scene: apart from lines, much better, Barbara – I can tell you're getting more used to the straitjacket. Oh – any news on the skull, Connie? I'm just thinking, if your little dog pulls through, we'll have to fall back on papier mâché. All right, Connie, as long as it's dead by the dress . . .

That's it for tonight then; thank you. I shall expect you all to be word-perfect by the next rehearsal. Have any of you realised what date we're up to? Yes, April the twenty-seventh! And when do we open? August! It's not long!

Victoria Wood
From *Up to You, Porky* (1985)

Song: *Moody Dane*

Moody Dane,
Moody Dane,
Why are
You moody?
Broody Dane,
Broody Dane,
Don't be
So broody!
Smile a smile, dear,
Dry your eyes,
Try not to
Soliloquize.
Don't keep sayin':
'That's the question,'
It is only
Indigestion –

Moody Dane,
Moody Dane,
Don't be
So naughty!
It is all
Wrong to call
Your Momma
Bawdy –
There's a bend in every lane,
Soon the sun will shine again,
Skies of blue come after rain,
Moody Dane,
Moody Dane.

Words by **Herbert Farjeon**
Music by **John Pritchett**
From the revue *Nine Sharp* (1938)

Rehearsing Hamlet

26 November 1975. Peter Hall records in his diary:

Tense atmosphere at *Hamlet* rehearsal this morning.
Poor Angela Lansbury has to leave tomorrow for
three days in Los Angeles as her mother has died.
Our rhythm of work disturbed. I tidied up a few
things, and then we went into the run-through. It
was not bad, slightly jumpy, slightly crude, things
which had long been secure going awry, Angela
obviously working under great strain. She came on
for Ophelia's death news and started the speech with
the most amazing emotional complexity. Then she
stopped; nearly went on; tried to control herself; tried
to go on. The silence lasted for ever. Everyone in the
cast felt the reality of death.

From *Peter Hall's Diaries* (1983)

Ian Charleson Plays Hamlet

Richard Eyre recalls another National Theatre Hamlet:

I had once talked to Ian Charleson about the parts he wanted to play – Richard II, Angelo, Benedick, Hamlet and – as he said to me – 'Lear, God willing.' He had a real passion for Shakespeare. He loved the density of thought, the great Shakespearean paradoxes, the lyricism, the energy of the verse. He didn't want to paraphrase it; for him the meaning was in the poetry and the poetry in the meaning.

When I asked him to play Hamlet I knew he'd been ill. He told me that he was HIV Positive. As we embarked on rehearsals he was having regular, and immensely painful acupuncture treatment, and later on chemotherapy which exhausted and debilitated him. Later in his illness he defiantly rejected all treatment; he wanted to be himself, however painful that was.

Shortly before his death, Hamlet says 'Since no man of aught he leaves knows aught, what is't to leave betimes? Let be.' Ian and I talked a great deal about Hamlet's accommodation with death, Ian's own state lurking just below the surface as hidden subtext. He was very fastidious about the 'Let be'. For him it wasn't a chiding of Horatio or a shrug of stoic indifference, it was an assertion, a proposed epitaph perhaps: don't fuss, don't panic, don't be afraid.

I've no idea if it was Kennedy's coinage, more likely one of his speech-writers, but the definition of courage as 'grace under pressure' was perfectly suited to Ian. In his last performance of *Hamlet* he acted as if he knew that it was the last time he'd be on stage. He hadn't played the previous two nights and was feeling guilty about what he saw as his lack of professionalism. 'If they pay you, you should turn up,' he said. By the end of the performance he was visibly exhausted, each line of his final scene painfully wrung from him, his farewell and the character's agonisingly merged. He stood at the curtain call like a tired boxer, battered by applause.

When he became unable to perform, it was a real deprivation to him. 'You know me,' he said 'if there are two people out there who I can impress, I'd be there if I could.' And he would, if he'd had the strength. We're often accused of sentimentality in the theatre, but it can't be sentimental to miss someone whose company gave so much joy, whose talent really *did* add to the sum of human happiness, and whose courage was beyond admiration.

I had a letter from him a few weeks before he died, just before Christmas. He said: 'One day when I'm better I'd love to attempt Hamlet again, and all the rest. I hope this is not a dream, and I can't tell you how much of a kick I got out of doing the part, if only for the short time I could . . . '

Let be.

Richard Eyre
From *Utopia and Other Places* (1993)

Song: *Fear No More*

Fear no more the heat o' th' sun
Nor the furious winter's rages,
Thou thy worldly task has done,
Home art gone and ta'en thy wages.
Golden lads and girls all must,
As chimney-sweepers, come to dust.

Fear no more the lightning-flash,
Nor th' all-dreaded thunder-stone,
Fear not slander, censure rash,
Thou hast finish'd joy and moan.
All lovers young, all lovers must
Consign to thee and come to dust.

Words by **William Shakespeare**
Music by **Stephen Sondheim**
From the musical *The Frogs* (1974)

Part Two

Song: **A Warwickshire Lad**

Ye Warwickshire lads and ye lasses
See what at our jubilee passes;
Come revel away, rejoice and be glad,
Come revel away, rejoice and be glad,
For the lad of all lads was a Warwickshire lad.

Warwickshire lad, all be glad,
For the lad of all lads was a Warwickshire lad.
Warwickshire lad, all be glad,
For the lad of all lads was a Warwickshire lad.

Be proud of the charms of your county,
Where nature has lavished her bounty;
Where much has been giv'n and some to be spared,
Where much has been giv'n and some to be spared,
For the bard of all bards was a Warwickshire bard.

Warwickshire bard, never compared,
For the bard of all bards was a Warwickshire bard.
Warwickshire bard, never compared,
For the bard of all bards was a Warwickshire bard.

Birthday Celebrations

My lords, ladies and gentlemen, on Shakespeare's
birthday in the year 1864, when the memory of
drama's great high priest is receiving the heart
homage of not only a nation, but almost a universe, I
find myself, a humble player, called upon to address
you all. You will pardon, I am sure, a confession of
pride from one who has the happy privilege of
making the study of Shakespeare's matchless works
the pleasant labour of his life.

I thank the committee for the honourable position
they have accorded in their programme to the
actor's art. It was David Garrick himself who led the
Shakespeare celebrations in 1769. They were sadly
marred by such torrential rain, that many avowed the
deluge was the judgement of the Great Ruler on an
idolatrous jubilee. Boswell reports that when the
chorus united in Dibdin's *Warwickshire Lad* they
were all but swept away by the swollen waters of the
usually soft-flowing Avon.

Mr Creswick (1864)

Song: *A Warwickshire Lad* (*Reprise*)

Our Shakespeare compared is to no man,
Nor Frenchman nor Grecian nor Roman;
Their swans are all geese to the Avon's sweet swan,
Their swans are all geese to the Avon's sweet swan,
For the man of all men was a Warwickshire man.

Warwickshire man, Avon's sweet swan,
For the man of all men was a Warwickshire man.
Warwickshire man, Avon's sweet swan,
For the man of all men was a Warwickshire man.

Charles Dibdin (1769)

Overlooked by Alan Howard, Michael Gambon does his Olivier impression.

So That's The Way You Like It

This is played with great vigour at tremendous speed in the modern Shakespeare style. The characters wear various period hats as required. Enter PETER.

PETER: Sustain we now description of a time
 When petty lust and overweening tyranny
 Offend the ruck of state.
 Thus fly we now, as oft with Phœbus did
 Fair Asterope, unto proud Flanders court.
 Where is the warlike Warwick,
 Like to the mole that sat on Hector's brow,
 Fairset for England and for war!

Enter JON *and* ALAN.

48

JON: And so we bid you welcome to our Court,
    Fair Cousin Albany and you our sweetest Essex
    Take this my hand, and you fair Essex this
    And with this bond we'll cry anon
    And shout Jack Cock of London to the Foe.
    Approach your ears and kindly bend your
        conscience to my piece,
    Our ruddy scouts to me this hefty news have
        brought:
    The naughty English, expecting now some
        pregnance in our plan,
    Have with some haughty purpose
    Bent Aeolis unto the service of their sail.
    So even now, while we to the wanton lute do
        strut,
    Is brutish Bolingbroke bent fair upon
    Some fickle circumstance.

ALAN *and* PETER: Some fickle circumstance.

JON: Get thee to Gloucester, Essex. Do thee to
        Wessex, Exeter,
    Fair Albany to Somerset must eke his route
    And Scroup do you to Westmoreland, where shall
        bold York
    Enrouted now for Lancaster, with forces of our
        Uncle Rutland,
    Enjoin his standard with sweet Norfolk's host.
    Fair Sussex, get thee to Warwicksbourne,
    And there, with frowning purpose, tell our plan
    To Bedford's tilted ear, that he shall press
    With most insensate speed
    And join his warlike effort to bold Dorset's side.
    I most royally shall now to bed,
    To sleep off all the nonsense I've just said.

**Alan Bennett, Peter Cook,
Jonathan Miller** and **Dudley Moore**
From the revue *Beyond The Fringe* (1960)

Mistress Quickly.   Linda Bassett.

Song: *Ladies of London*

ALL: We're ladies of London, as you very well can see,

TEARSHEET: Doll Tearsheet,

COMMON: Doll Common,

OVERDONE: Doll Overdone

QUICKLY: And me.

ALL: Oh well may you ask us just what's going on –
We're off to the funeral of Merry Sir John.
We all clubbed together for flowers for his hearse
As soon as we heard Sir John Falstaff was worse.

TEARSHEET: He promised me money,

COMMON: He promised me gold,

OVERDONE: He promised to marry me when he grew
old,

QUICKLY: He promised to pay and got credit did he,
from

TEARSHEET: Doll Tearsheet,

COMMON: Doll Common,

OVERDONE: Doll Overdone

QUICKLY: And me.

ALL: We're ladies of London and we ought to know;
They don't come more Christian from Bankside to
Bow.

TEARSHEET: He may have been fat,

COMMON: And he was scant of breath,

OVERDONE: But somehow it's 'ard to believe in his
death;

QUICKLY: 'Cause all of his life he behaved a bit free

TEARSHEET: With Tearsheet,

COMMON: And Common,

OVERDONE: And Overdone

QUICKLY: And me.

ALL: We're ladies of London, and it won't be the
same;
He was sprightly twice nightly, and lord was he
game.

TEARSHEET: He owed for his drink,

COMMON: And he owed for his rent,

OVERDONE: He owed for his shirt, but we're sorry he
went.

ALL: We'll do all we can for Sir John's memoree

TEARSHEET: Will Tearsheet,

COMMON: And Common,

OVERDONE: And Overdone

QUICKLY: And me.

Words by **Caryl Brahms** and **Ned Sherrin**
From the musical *No Bed For Bacon* (1959)
Music by **Malcolm McKee** (1994)

The Repertory Actor

The repertory actor earns
   My very high respect,
For think of all the parts he learns
   And has to recollect;
And when he acts in Shakespeare's plays
   His life's an almost hopeless maze.

On Monday, as Antonio,
   He dodges Shylock's knife;
On Tuesday, being Prospero
   He leads the simple life;
On Wednesday he must go to death
   As Lear, on Friday as Macbeth.

At Thursday's matinee he's made
   To play the fool and chaff
As Touchstone, or as Quince he's paid
   To make the children laugh;
At night he must appear again
   To play the melancholy Dane.

Oh, why is Romeo amazed?
   Why does he turn his back
On Juliet, and look so dazed . . . ?

Guy Boas (1925)

Wherefore Art Thou Juliet?

*We hear a snatch of the love theme from
Tchaikovsky's* Romeo and Juliet.

ACTOR: But soft! What light from yonder window
    breaks?
It is the east, and Juliet is the sun!
It is my lady; O, it is my love!

ACTRESS: The raven himself is hoarse
That croaks the fatal entrance of Duncan
Under my battlements.

ACTOR: (It's not Duncan, dear, it's Romeo.)

ACTRESS: (What?)

ACTOR: (It's Tuesday.)

ACTRESS: (Never mind, carry on.)

ACTOR: She speaks:
O, speak again bright angel. For thou art
As glorious to this night, being o'er my head,
As a winged messenger of heaven.

ACTRESS: Come to my woman's breasts
And take my milk for gall.

ACTOR: (Oh my God.)
I am too bold, 'tis not to me she speaks.

ACTRESS: Come, thick night,
And pall me in the dunnest smoke of hell,
That my keen knife see not the wound it makes.

ACTOR: See, how she leans her cheek upon her hand!
O, that I were a glove upon that hand,

That I might touch that cheek.

ACTRESS: I have given suck.

ACTOR: (For heaven's sake!)

Knocking heard

ACTRESS: I hear a knocking
At the south entry. Retire we to our chamber.

ACTOR: With love's light wings did I o'er perch
   these walls,
For stony limits cannot hold love out.

ACTRESS: I have given suck.

ACTOR: (I keep telling you, woman, this is Tuesday.
   You give suck on Wednesdays.)

ACTRESS: What, will these hands ne'er be clean?
Here's the smell of blood still.

ACTOR: Henceforth I never will be Romeo.

ACTRESS: Fie, my lord, fie, a soldier and afeard?

Knocking heard

To bed, to bed, there's knocking at the gate.
Get on your nightgown, lest occasion call us.

ACTOR: I am afeard all this is but a dream,
Too flattering-sweet to be substantial.

Knocking heard

ACTRESS: Wash your hands, look not so pale.
What's done cannot be undone. To bed, to bed, to
   bed.

ACTOR: I have no joy of this contract tonight.

Alan Melville
From the revue *For Amusement Only* (1956)

Song: *Cravin' for the Avon*

My poor heart is cravin' for Stratford-on-Avon,
Where all my loves appear in plays by Will
   Shakespeare,
From Caesar to King Lear.

There's nothin' that I wouldn't do for
A nice hunk of a man like Macbeth;
Othello's a fellow I'd queue for,
He could just squeeze me to death.
King John is a king that I'm gone on,
For Richard III my heart stops,
With a hey nonny hey, and a hey nonny no,
And Bottom is simply the tops.

CHORUS
Cravin' for the Avon,
Stratford is a haven,
Rantin' and a-ravin',
Cravin' for the Avon.

For an evening with Orlando I would even say
   to Brando
'Call around some other night.'
And I'm sure I'd understand ya better than your
   Queen Titania,
Oberon my favourite sprite!
That wicked first murderer slays me,
Mercutio is ever so cute,
With a hey nonny hey, and a hey nonny no,
And Brutus a beautiful brute.
Ooo!

CHORUS
Cravin' for the Avon,
Stratford is a haven,
Rantin' and a-ravin',
Cravin' for the Avon.

Oh, no!
Shakespeare, Shakespeare give me the works!
Give me the works of Shakespeare.
Cravin' for the Avon, cravin' for the Avon,
    cravin' for the Avon.
Shakespeare!

Words by **James Gilbert**
Music by **Julian More**
From the musical *Grab Me A Gondola* (1956)

William and the Lost Tourist

William wandered home from school, running over in his mind the speech from Shakespeare he had been told to learn by his English master: 'Friends, Rome and Countrymen, lend me some ears, I come to bury Caesar in his grave.'

Suddenly, he spotted a car at the corner of the road, and in the car was a weeping young woman. William stood and gaped. The weeping young woman was astonishingly beautiful, and William, in spite of his professed scorn of the feminine sex, was very susceptible to beauty. William blinked and coughed. The young woman turned sapphire-blue swimming eyes to him and gulped.

'Say, kid,' she said, with an American twang and intonation that completed the enslavement of William, 'say, kid, what's the name of this lil' old town?'

William was too much confused to reply for a moment. During that moment fresh tears welled up in the blue eyes.

'I feel jus' like *nothing*. I've lost the way an' I've lost the map an' I don't know where I've got to.'

'Where did you want to get to?'

'Stratford. Stratford-upon-Avon, that Shakespeare guy's place. If I don't do it today I'll never do it. Everyone I know's done it an' to go back home an' say I've not seen Stratford – well, I'd never hold my head up again – *never* – and I've lost the way and the map and – '

She ended in a sob that reduced William's already melting heart to complete liquefaction.

'It's all right.'

He didn't mean anything in particular. It was only a vague expression of sympathy and comfort.

'You mean this *is* Stratford? Oh, how *dandy*. Do you really mean that?'

Stronger and older characters than William would have decided to mean that when fixed by those pleading blue eyes.

'Yes, this is Stratford all right.'

'Say, kid, I jus' *adore* you. Now I've got to see it *all* jus' as quick as I can.'

She opened the door and jumped down.

'Now the first thing I wanna see is Anne Hathaway's cottage. Would you be a reel cherub, and personally conduct me?'

'Yes, I would.'

William did not repent his rash statement. If this vision wished it to be Stratford it *was* Stratford.

They set off down the road together.

'Is it far?'

'Well, whose cottage did you say?'

'Anne Hathaway's.'

'Oh, no, it's not far now.'

The lady became confidential. She told him that her name was Miss Burford – Sadie Burford.

'I jus' *love* this lil' ole country. I've *longed* so *passionately* to see Stratford; this is the happiest day of my life.'

They turned the bend in the road and there in front of them was Mrs Maloney's cottage. Mrs Maloney lived alone with a dog and a cat and a canary. She was very old and very cantankerous.

William firmly believed her to be a witch. Miss Burford gave a little scream of ecstasy.

'*Thatched*. This must be Anne Hathaway's cottage.'

'Yes, this is it. And there's Anne Hathaway looking out of the window.'

'Does an Anne Hathaway *still* live here?'

'Well I thought that was what you said.'

'But I meant the one that lived hundreds of years ago.'

'She'll be dead by now.'

But if she wanted an Anne whatever it was, she should have one.

'There's another living there now.'

'How *dandy*. A descendant, I suppose?'

'Oh, yes. Yes – that's what she is.'

'Well, will you knock, or shall I?'

'You – you don't want to go *right* in, do you?'

'I sure do.'

'I – I wouldn't if I was you. She's *awfully* bad-tempered, Mrs Maloney is – I mean Anne what you said is.'

'But I must go in – people *do,* I know.'

'But she's mad – she's sort of forgotten her name – she – she sort of thinks she's someone else. It's best from outside. It's not anything like as nice inside as it is outside.'

'But I've known people who've gone inside.'

She advanced boldly and knocked on the door. William stood in the background palely composed, but ready to flee if necessary. The door opened a few inches and Mrs Maloney's wrinkled face appeared round it. At the sight of William it became distorted with rage.

'Ah-h-h.' she growled. 'Ye little pest, ye –'

'Could I – could I just look at your historical cottage, Miss Hathaway?'

''Ysterical yourself, an' me name's Mrs Maloney, I'd have ye to know.'

Miss Burford turned to William with a sad smile.

'Poor woman.'

Then she entered the kitchen.Miss Burford looked round the old-fashioned cottage, the old dresser and the flagged floor with a sigh of rapture.

'How lovely. How perfect. But I had an idea there were more things in it.'

'There were a lot more things, but they had to take them away when she – when she got like this.'

'Eh? What's he saying?'

'Nothing, nothing.'

Miss Burford, throwing dignity to the winds, followed William's already fleeing figure.

'Poor woman. She's sure plumb crazy. But I can say I've seen it now. That's all I wanted to do.'

She took from her pocket a little note-book, opened it and ticked off 'Stratford' and 'Anne Hathaway's Cottage'.

'I suppose there aren't any other of his folks about the place – kind of descendants, you know?'

'There's me. I'm one of his folks.'

He was secretly aghast when he heard himself say that. But he merely continued to gaze at her with his most ingenuous expression.

'Well, now. Isn't that jus' *luck*. You're one of his descendants? *Fancy. Fancy* that. I guess I was lucky to strike *you* first go off. What's your name?'

'William.'

'Of course, after him. Of course.'

When Miss Burford returned home, she gave a little lecture on her English travels. She told of her visit to Anne Hathaway's cottage, whose present occupant was very old and suffering from senile decay. She told how in the same town she met a descendant of Shakespeare.

'It was wonderful, wasn't it?'

Her lecture was a great success.

That Christmas, one Christmas card was sent to William that never reached him. It was sent from America, and was addressed to 'Master William Shakespeare, Stratford-upon-Avon, England'.

Richmal Crompton
From *William The Conqueror* (1926)

Comedy of Errors — R.S.C. Stratford
Antipholus (Desmond Barrit)

Mark Thompson '90

Song: **Teach Me, Dear Creature**

Teach me, dear creature, how to think and speak.
Lay open to my earthly gross conceit,
Smothered in errors, feeble, shallow, weak,
The folded meaning of your word's deceit.
Against my soul's pure truth why labour you
To make it wander in an unknown field?
Are you a god? Would you create me new?
Transform me, then, and to your power I'll yield.

O, train me not, sweet mermaid, with thy note
To drown me in thy sister's flood of tears.
Sing, siren, for thyself, and I will dote.
Spread o'er the silver waves thy golden hairs
And as a bed I'll take thee, and there lie,
And in that glorious supposition think
He gains by death that hath such means to die.
Let love, being light, be drownèd if she sink.

Words by **William Shakespeare**
Music by **Julian Slade**
From the musical *The Comedy of Errors* (1954)

Seeing Stratford

There was one moment in Stratford the other afternoon when I really did feel I was treading upon Shakespeare's own ground. It was in the gardens of New Place, very brave in the spring sunlight. You could have played the outdoor scene of *Twelfth Night* in them without disturbing a leaf. There was the very sward for Viola and Sir Andrew. Down that paved path Olivia would come, like a great white peacock. Against that bank of flowers the figure of Maria would be seen, flitting like a starling. The little Knott Garden alone was worth the journey and nearer to Shakespeare than all the documents and chairs and monuments. I remember that when we left that garden to see the place where Shakespeare was buried, it didn't seem to matter much. Why should it when we had just seen the place where he was still alive?

J.B. Priestley
From *Apes and Angels* (1927)

Theatre Visitors

In the stage-struck days of my youth, it was for the
Royal Shakespeare Theatre that I came to Stratford
and I rarely strayed far from its precincts. I have only
to push open the heavy glass doors and step inside
that cool, rather imposing and formal area, and sniff,
and I am sixteen again, the queue in which I have
been standing for over an hour has at last got within
sight of the box office.

There was tremendous camaraderie among those
queueing for standing tickets or returns – I imagine
there still is; you meet and make firm friends with
people standing next to you, from Ohio or Tokyo,
Stockholm or Tipperary, swop anecdotes about plays
seen, pin-ups among this year's actors, and then part,
abruptly, never to see one another again.

An air of excitement, of anticipation and
participation, those are what the theatre generates. If
there is ever a sense of Shakespeare being a man
dead and lost in history, then the life of the theatre
which exists to present his plays dispels all that,
brings the man and his work into the world as it is
now, a new creation every season. Shakespeare lives!

Susan Hill
From *Shakespeare Country* (1987)

The Forest of Arden

In 1970 the RSC asked me – Maureen Lipman – to
audition for Celia in Buzz Goodbody's production of
As You Like It. It was a part that was small enough
and possibly characterful enough for me to wrestle
away my Shakespeare demons in a quiet way, out in
the country. Or so I thought.

I left my husband of six weeks and headed
Warwickshirewards. I moved into delightful lodgings
in the Old Town, with beamed ceiling and matching
landlady, and turned my attentions to Bardomania.

The set for *As You Like It* was modishly abstract.
The Forest of Arden was represented by a large,
circular white carpet, on which all the action took
place, and a ceiling full of long tubes of steel of
varying lengths tied up by string, and capable of
shifting to any number of positions to represent
either a forest, a court or a ceiling full of steel tubes.
Never has the line 'So *this* is the Forest of Arden?' had
a more comic intonation.

Maureen Lipman
From *How Was It For You ?* (1985)

68

Anecdotage

There was a woman watching *Macbeth* at Stratford who leant forward, tapping a friend on the shoulder, to say, 'So now do you see how one lie leads to another?'

Another woman, leaving a performance of *Antony and Cleopatra* was overheard saying 'Yes, and the funny thing is exactly the same thing happened to Monica.'

Then there was the experience of Sarah Bernhardt's portrayal of Cleopatra at the end of the last century. This reached a violent and devastating climax in which she tore round her palace, wrecking everything in sight, and finally collapsed amongst the debris littering the stage. The audience loved it and frequently rewarded her efforts with a standing ovation. One night, however, an elderly patron was led from her seat after the final curtain, remarking 'How different, how very different, from the home life of our own dear Queen.'

During an American tour of *A Midsummer Night's Dream,* no suitable theatre was to be found at one of the bookings, so the company performed in a floodlit sports arena. Sir Robert Helpmann, as Oberon, was given the umpire's dressing-room, the nearest the stage manager could find to those usually allocated to the star. When he went round to call the half-hour, there was no reply from the umpire's dressing-room, so he opened the door to check that the actor was there. He was, albeit a little preoccupied.

The stage manager found Robert Helpmann standing on a chair, which was itself standing on a table, craning his face towards the solitary lightbulb hanging from the ceiling as he applied his elaborate green and gold eye make-up.

'Are you all right up there?' asked the stage manager, with some alarm.

'Oh, yes, I'm fine,' said the star looking down. 'But heaven knows how these umpires manage.'

Sir Donald Wolfit's touring company included a young actor whose aspirations sadly outstripped his ability. Wolfit cast him as Seyton in *Macbeth*, entrusting him with the news of Lady Macbeth's demise: 'The queen, my lord, is dead.' He played this for several seasons until it started to bore him and he asked Wolfit for a larger part. Wolfit declined. The actor continued asking and Wolfit stuck to his guns. Into this stalemate came thoughts of revenge. When *Macbeth* was next performed he ran on stage as usual and in answer to Macbeth's question 'Wherefore was that cry?' answered, 'My lord, the queen is much better and is even now at dinner.'

Derek Nimmo
From *As The Actress Said To The Bishop* (1989)

Song: *The Night I Appeared as Macbeth*

'Twas thro' a Y.M.C.A. concert
I craved a desire for the stage.
In Frinton one night, I was asked to recite,
Gadzooks, I was quickly the rage.
They said I was better than Irving,
And gave me some biscuits and tea,
I know it's not Union wages,
But that was the usual fee.
Home I came, bought some dress,
Appeared in your theatre and what a success.

I acted so tragic the house rose like magic,
The audience yelled 'You're sublime!'
They made me a present of Mornington Crescent,
They threw it a brick at a time.
Someone threw a fender which caught me a bender,
I hoisted a white flag and tried to surrender,
They jeered me, they queered me,
And half nearly stoned me to death.
They threw nuts and sultanas, fried eggs and bananas
The night I appeared as Macbeth.

The advertised time for the curtain
Was six forty-five on the sheet.
The hall keeper he having mislaid the key,
We played the first act in the street.
Then somebody called for the author,
'He's dead' said the flute-player's wife –
The news caused an awful commotion,
And gave me the shock of my life.
Shakespeare dead, dear old Bill,
Why I never knew the poor fellow was ill.

I acted so tragic the house rose like magic,
They wished David Garrick could see.
But he's in the Abbey, then someone quite shabby
Suggested that's where I should be.
I withdrew my sabre, and started to labour,
Cried 'Lay on Macduff' to my swashbuckle
    neighbour,
I hollered 'I'm collared, and I must
Reach the bridge or it's death!'
But they altered my journey, I reached the infirm'ry
The night I appeared as Macbeth.

William Hargreaves (1922)

MACBETH: "FILTHY HAGS! WHY DO YOU SHOW ME THIS? — A FOURTH? — START, EYES! — WHAT WILL THE LINE STRETCH OUT TO TH' CRACK OF DOOM? — ANOTHER YET..."

The Verse Problem

Of all the problems which *Macbeth* poses, none is more critical to the Shakespearean actor than the verse problem. Unfortunately, nobody is quite sure what the Verse Problem is exactly. Suffice it to say, however, that it causes havoc in numerous regional and West End theatres and can usually be spotted by a number of 'tell-tale symptoms' such as contrapuntal off-beats, dissonant rhyming mechanisms, alliterative assonants and, worst of all, irregular vowel movements, which can cause serious, not to say agonising, problems for the emergent actor.

Here anyway are some 'Useful Exercises when Attempting Verse':
1. Keep Calm.
2. Lie on the floor and take three deep breaths followed by 149 short breaths without pause for three hours.
3. Shake out ankles, rib cage and lower intestine and above all – *relax*!

Things to Do:
1. Make a scale model of 'The Dawning of the Elizabethan Epoch'.
2. Caper nimbly in a lady's chamber.

Patrick Barlow
From *Shakespeare: the Truth* (1993)

Exam Questions

Before next week's lecture I'd like you to consider the following questions:

1. One of the sword fights in *Henry V* includes the stage direction 'they draw on both sides'. Was there a shortage of paper at Agincourt?

2. Some scholars maintain that Juliet had no balcony. Did she have a bay window?

3. If you were Hamlet, would it give you comic relief to hold in your hands the skull of an old friend?

Richard Armour
From *Twisted Tales From Shakespeare* (1957)

Song: *Give Us A Rest*

Trio for HAMLET, JULIET and HENRY V

ALL: We don't need an introduction
    – more's the pity!
We're afraid we're quite familiar
    to you all.
Our time-honoured conversation's
Simply bursting with quotations
Which you poor things had to
    learn when you were small.
We're appearing here tonight
    to make it cle-ar
That though you may be tired of us
You can't be half as tired as we are.

Give us a rest, we implore you.
Give us a rest is all our plea.
We're fed up with being acted
And we'd like to be subtracted
From the repertoire of ev'ry company.
We feel we've done our duty by the public
And we know we've always given of our best,

JULIET: But Romeo and I would love to get to know
    our grave.

HENRY V: And both my arms are aching from this
    sword I have to wave.

HAMLET: And I've begun to realise why I'm called a
    peasant slave.

ALL: Give us a rest, give us a rest, give us a rest.

76

HAMLET: I'm encored
But I'm bored,
And I'm retiring to the closet indisposed.

JULIET: I am sick
Of the Vic,
And I've a notice on my balcony which says 'We
never closed'.

HENRY V: I'm so madly patriotic
That it's making me neurotic,
And I'm sick of climbing through that ruddy breech.

ALL: We've been done upon the stage, on the radio
and the screen.

JULIET: I've been done by girls of forty when I'm
s'posed to be fourteen.

ALL: We've been done in sev'ral periods which we
found extremely weird.

HAMLET: I've been done by Alec Guinness in a rather
nasty beard.

ALL: Peter Brook and Tyrone Guthrie, Donald Wolfit
and the lot
Have used us to express we're never sure exactly
what,
And if none of us rebels
We'll be done by Orson Welles,
So please forgive us, if we beseech –

Give us a rest – are you list'ning?
Give us a rest – or shoot us dead!
And for heaven's sake protect us
From those Amazon directors,
Let them loose on *Lear* or *Pericles* instead.

HAMLET AND HENRY V: We've both of us been done by Mr Branagh,

HAMLET: And once was quite enough, I would suggest.

JULIET: We're going to make a stand, no matter what it may involve.

HAMLET: And in the last resort to go on strike is our resolve –

HENRY V: Before young Daldry puts us on the National's revolve –

Juliet screams

ALL: Give us a rest!
Give us a rest!
Give us a rest!

Sandy Wilson
From the revue *See You Later* (1953)
Additional lyrics (1994)

The Curtain

When the curtain goes down at the end of the play,
The actors and actresses hurry away.

Titania, Bottom and Quince, being stars,
Can afford to drive home in their own private cars.

Hippolyta, Starveling and Flute are in luck,
They've been offered a lift in a taxi by Puck;

And Snug and Lysander and Oberon pop
In a bus, and Demetrius clambers on top.

With a chorus of fairies no bus can compete,
So they are obliged to trudge home on their feet.

It seems rather hard on the poor little things,
After flying about all the evening with wings.

Guy Boas (1925)

Song: *Brush Up Your Shakespeare*

Brush up your Shakespeare,
Start quoting him now.
Brush up your Shakespeare,
And the women you will wow.
Better mention *The Merchant of Venice*
When her sweet pound of flesh you would menace.
If her virtue at first she defends well,
Just remind her that *All's Well that Ends Well*.
And if still she won't give you a bonus
You know what Venus got from Adonis.

And here are some GCSE answers from local schools:
– In *Macbeth* the witches are evil people. They are
   the representatives of Satin.
– How did the witches know that Macbeth was going
   to be Thane or Corder? Did they ask around?
– One of Shakespeare's plays is called *Charley's
   Aunt*.

Brush up your Shakespeare,
And they'll all kow-tow.

Brush up your Shakespeare,
Start quoting him now.
Brush up your Shakespeare,
And the women you will wow.
With the wife of the British Ambessida,
Try a crack out of *Troilus and Cressida*.
If she says your behaviour is heinous,
Kick her right in the *Coriolanus*.
When your baby is pleading for pleasure,
Let her sample your *Measure for Measure*.

– In *The Tempest* one of the main characters is
  Prospero, who has a daughter called Veranda.
– Nobody would know Romeo was a Capulet
  because everyone would be carefully keeping their
  faeces covered.
– Some of Shakespeare's plays are written in heroic
  cutlets.
– Shakespeare married Anne Hathaway, but he
  mostly lived at Windsor with his merry wives. This
  is quite usual with actors.

Brush up your Shakespeare,
And they'll all kow-tow.
Thinks thou?
And they'll all kow-tow.
Odds bodkins.
They'll all kow-tow.

Cole Porter
From the musical *Kiss Me Kate* (1948)
Classroom Howlers by children
who prefer to remain anonymous

Curtain Speech

SIR: My Lords, Ladies and Gentlemen. Thank you
for the manner in which you have received the
greatest tragedy in our language. We live in
dangerous times. Our civilisation is under threat
from the forces of darkness, and we, humble
actors, do all in our power to fight as soldiers
on the side of right in the great battle. Our most
cherished ambition is to keep alive the best of our
drama, to serve the greatest poet-dramatist who
has ever lived, by taking his plays to every corner
of our beloved island. Tomorrow night we shall
give –

NORMAN: *Richard III.*

SIR:– *King Richard III.* I myself will play the
hunchback king. On Saturday afternoon my lady
wife will play –

NORMAN: Portia.

SIR: – Portia, and I the badly-wronged Jew in *The
Merchant of Venice*, a play you may think of
greater topicality than ever. On Saturday night –

NORMAN: *Lear.*

SIR: – On Saturday night we shall essay once more
the tragedy you have this evening witnessed, and
I myself shall again undergo the severest test
known to an actor. Next week, God willing, we
shall be in –

NORMAN: Eastbourne.

SIR: – Eastbourne. I trust your friends and relatives

there will, on your kind recommendation, discover
source for refreshment, as you seem to have done
by your warm indication, in the glorious words we
are privileged to speak. For the generous manner
in which you have received our earnest
endeavours, on behalf of my lady wife, my
company and myself, I remain your humble and
obedient servant, and can no other answer make
but thanks and thanks, and ever thanks.

Ronald Harwood
From *The Dresser* (1980)

THE DRESSER
TOM COURTENAY *as Norman*
FREDDIE JONES *as Sir*

Song: *That Shakespearian Rag*

'Friends, Romans, Countrymen,
I come not here to praise,'
But lend an ear and you will hear
A rag, yes, a rag that is grand, and
Bill Shakespeare never knew
Of ragtime in his days,
But the high browed rhymes,
Of his syncopated lines,
You'll admit, surely fit, any song that's now a hit,
So this rag, I submit.

CHORUS
That Shakespearian rag,
Most intelligent, very elegant,
That old classical drag,
Has the proper stuff, the line 'Lay on Macduff',
Desdemona was Othello's pet,
Romeo loved his Juliet
And they were some lovers, you can bet, and yet,
I know if they were here today,
They'd Grizzly Bear in a different way,
And you'd hear old Hamlet say,
'To be or not to be'
That Shakespearian Rag.

Words by **Gene Buck** and **Herman Ruby**
Music by **David Stamper**
From *The Ziegfeld Follies of 1912*

Song: **Let's Do It**

Mr Irving Berlin often emphasised sin
In a charming way.
Mr Coward we know wrote a song or two to
   show
Love was here to stay.
Cole Porter it's true took a sentimental view
Of that sly biological urge;
But Shakespeare was the first
To really make the whole thing merge.

He wrote that:
Ladies do it, Lords do it,
Even ravening hordes do it –
Let's do it, let's fall in love.
Queen Gertrude twice in a trice did it,
King Lear evidently thrice did it –
Let's do it, let's fall in love.

We're told that Henry V did it
With his happy few;
Lady Macbeth did it,
And Macbeth did it too.
Juliet stayed up late to do it,
Poor Miranda couldn't wait to do it –
Let's do it, let's fall in love.

In the spring of each year inhibitions disappear
And our hearts leap high.
To Stratford we go (hey nonny nonny no)
With this alibi:
To commune with the Bard in his very own
    back yard,
The temptation is oh so strong;
But before very long
Nature's singing us the same old song.

'Cos leading ladies having flings do it,
Extras waiting in the wings do it –
Let's do it, let's fall in love.
Young men clutching spears do it,
Young girls, frequently in tears, do it –
Let's do it, let's fall in love.
Some rather seasoned old pro's do it
When they get a bit tight;
The cast of *King Lear* do it
(But it takes them all night).
Those handsome leading men do it,
Designers make a model and then do it –
Let's do it, let's fall in love.

All my friends claim they don't do it,
I asked the pianist but he won't do it –
Let's do it, let's fall in love.
Green Room girls serving stew do it,
Certain members of the Crew do it –
Let's do it, let's fall in love.

Ladies in the Wardrobe do it
Given half a chance;
Friends of the RSC do it
If they book in advance.
All directors tell you how to do it,
I'd better rush home now to do it –
Let's do it, let's fall in love.

Dance Break

Critics in the dark do it,
Then they phone it through;
Box Office staff do it.
No they don't – oh yes they do.
All the names in this file do it,
One day maybe even I'll do it –
Let's do it, let's fall in love.

All those girls up in Wigs do it,
People sitting in their digs do it –
Let's do it, let's fall in love.
That pair there in Row A do it,
My dresser says he may do it –
Let's do it, let's fall in love.
RSC actors, when they do it,
Like to do it in verse;
Mr and Mrs Noble do it
(But they had to rehearse).
And now we hope you'll no longer question
The validity of our suggestion:
Let's do it, let's fall in love.

Cole Porter
From the musical *Paris* (1927)
Additional lyrics by **Noël Coward** (1934)
Further lyrics by **Linda Bassett**
and **Christopher Luscombe** (1991)

Appendix

Staging and Background Information

The original staging of the revue was simple and flexible. There were five performers: three male and two female, one of the actors doubling as pianist. Four chairs and the piano formed an arc at the rear of the stage, with a performance space in front. Initially presented for one Sunday evening, the revue was partly learnt (musical numbers and sketches) and partly read (monologues, stories etc.). The items stood on their own without introduction. Below we describe the approach we took to each piece, but hope future directors will feel free to take what they want from this and discard the rest. We also include some background information on the authors and their material.

Part One

Prologue

After the briefest of overtures, the opening item was divided amongst the company, the quotations being separated into groups by snatches of music. These, like the overture, were taken from well-known musicals inspired by Shakespeare – *Kiss Me Kate, The Boys From Syracuse* and *West Side Story*. The unattributed quotation is by H.K. Bunner.

Quoting Shakespeare

We first encountered this piece as an RSC voice exercise, but it seems to work equally well as an introduction to the revue. Again, this was shared by all the actors, with the last line spoken in unison.

Brush Up Your Shakespeare

Cole Porter at first resisted the idea of a musical based on
The Taming of the Shrew, although he had frequently
referred to Shakespeare in earlier works. In 1935 he wrote
'As Juliet cried in Romeo's ear, / "Romeo, why not face the
fact, my dear?" ' – the fact being that it was *Just One of
Those Things*. The musical that emerged in 1948 as *Kiss Me
Kate* ran for 1,077 performances on Broadway, making
it Porter's most successful show. In 1987 it was successfully revived by the RSC in a production directed by Adrian
Noble. Perhaps the most obvious candidate for inclusion
in the revue, this number is only used for its opening
lines here, to set up the next piece. The rest of the song
follows in Part Two. It was sung in unison by the cast.

Who was William Shakespeare?

This extract is taken from the seminal study by Desmond
Olivier Dingle, alter ego of Patrick Barlow and founding
director of the National Theatre of Brent. He has said
that he hopes it will be 'not only a guide, manual and
reference work, but also a deep source of inspiration'.
Again, shared and read by the company.

The Music Hall Shakespeare

A classic example of the fascination which Shakespeare
has always had for the popular stage, this song was written
by Worton David, whose other successes included *I Want
to Sing in Opera* and *Hello, Hello, Who's Your Lady Friend?*
The music for the choruses was composed variously by
David himself, C.W. Murphy, Harry Castling and Dan
Lipton, while the music for the verses was written by Harry
Fragson. An Anglo-French artiste, Fragson performed his
prodigious repertoire of over three hundred songs at
music halls in London and Paris. In 1913, at the age of
forty-four, he suffered the unusual fate of being shot dead
by his Belgian father, his funeral being attended by an
estimated 20,000 people. Shortly after Fragson's death,
his widow, Alice Delysia, established herself in London
as a major star in a string of hit revues produced by

C.B. Cochran. In our staging the verses were sung/spoken as solos with the company joining in the choruses.

Othello

Leon 'Shakespeare' Cortez, popular on radio and in variety in the forties and fifties, retold the stories of many Shakespeare plays. The published editions of his work proudly reproduce a letter from the British Empire Shakespeare Society congratulating him on his portrayal of the 'frailties and humanities' of Shakespeare's characters. This extract from *Othello*, suggested to us by Roy Hudd, was performed in the revue as a solo stand-up act, flowing naturally from the previous item.

Who is Silvia?

Probably the most famous setting of any Shakespeare song, this version of Proteus' lyric from *The Two Gentlemen of Verona* was composed two years before Schubert's death. In the same month he produced two other Shakespeare songs: 'Hark, hark the lark' from *Cymbeline* and 'Come, thou monarch of the vine' from *Antony and Cleopatra*.

I'm in the RSC!

It should be pointed out that this item is not autobiographical. Jack Klaff appeared in the 1977 RSC Season, not spear-carrying, but playing a variety of substantial roles, and wrote this poem four years later for Dillie Keane, who suggested it to us. It has been performed on many occasions in many versions, usually by women, although it underwent a sex change in our production. Despite his unsparingly satirical view of the RSC, the author did return to Stratford in 1992.

Witches' Brew

The melody for this number was first heard under the title *Call Me Savage* in the 1964 musical *Fade Out – Fade In*, sung by Carol Burnett. Jule Styne recycled it in *Hallelujah, Baby!*, to create a ludicrously extravagant musical-within-a-musical. This Broadway version of the cauldron scene from *Macbeth* was an opportunity for our cast to indulge all their wildest Bob Fosse fantasies. We have reinstated some of Shakespeare's original words in place of the reworked Comden and Green lyrics, the latter requiring a knowledge of the plot. The verse segued into . . .

Which Witch?

This number became a hit for Hermione Gingold, and was revived by her in Alan Melville's series of *Sweet and Low* revues at the Ambassadors Theatre in the 1940s. We found various versions of the lyrics incorporating topical references to Dames Peggy, Edith and Sybil, Winston Churchill, Michael Foot, etc. The director addressed in the original was John Gielgud, and in Melville's subsequent recording he was replaced by Peter Hall. Our reference to Adrian Noble thus seemed permissable. The Australian composer Charles Zwar came to London in 1937 and began his long revue career at the Gate Theatre before the War. Melville was equally prolific: apart from television and radio credits, he wrote extensively for the stage – musicals, comedies and revues, including *A La Carte, At the Lyric, Six of One* and a retrospective programme *Déjà Revue* (1974).

Actors Prepare

This extract is taken from *Portrait of a Stratford Year,* which was first read at the 1985 Stratford-upon-Avon Poetry Festival by Tony Church and Richard Pasco. Roger Pringle is Director of the Shakespeare Centre in Stratford.

Shakespeare Masterclass

The speech under discussion here is spoken by Ulysses in Act III Scene 3 of *Troilus and Cressida*: 'Time hath, my lord, a wallet at his back, / Wherein he puts alms for oblivion.' The sketch was originally performed by the writers themselves in the 1981 Cambridge Footlights Revue. The cast also included Emma Thompson and Tony Slattery. Probably the most successful Footlights revue since the 1960s, it won the Perrier Award at Edinburgh and was subsequently televised. It was the first revue to be directed by a woman (Jan Ravens) in a hundred years of Footlights history.

The Coarse Actor

The Art of Coarse Acting is one of a series of comic manuals by Michael Green, including *The Art of Coarse Rugby* and *The Art of Coarse Golf.* His *Plays for Coarse Actors* include the Shakespeare parodies *All's Well That Ends As You Like It* and *Henry the Tenth (Part Seven).* Green took four Coarse Acting plays to the Edinburgh Festival in 1977, and two years later another collection transferred to the Shaftesbury Theatre in London.

Swap a Jest

The 1962 Footlights Revue (directed by Trevor Nunn) featured a parody of modern comics in a music hall setting, and as Tim Brooke-Taylor recalls, the following year this sketch emerged – the same characters, the same clichéd stand-up jokes, but this time translated to Shakespeare's Globe. *Cambridge Circus* was the most successful of all Footlights Revues, transferring to the West End and Broadway. It launched the careers of Brooke-Taylor, Bill Oddie, John Cleese, Graham Chapman, Jonathan Lynn and the producers Humphrey Barclay and David Hatch. Because of its London run, *Cambridge Circus* was unable to fulfil its touring obligations; these dates were taken on by a scratch Footlights company featuring Eric Idle and Richard Eyre.

Look Behind You, Hamlet!

Neither Frank Muir nor Denis Norden could find a script for this sketch, but it transpired that with uncanny foresight one of the original stars, June Whitfield, had kept a copy in her attic for the last forty years. *Take It From Here* ran from 1948 to 1959 and established the writing team of Muir and Norden, who occasionally appeared in the show under the mutual pseudonym of 'Herbert Mostyn', a combination of their middle names. The Glums were first heard in 1953 and eventually dominated the programme with Ron's

long-standing engagement to Eth, ever-interrupted by
Jimmy Edwards' Pa. The other cast members mentioned
here were David Dunhill ('Forward, Dunners') and 'Master'
Dick Bentley. This *Hamlet* parody belongs to the tradition
of Shakespeare burlesques which reached its peak in the
last century. Our cast performed it with scripts around a
microphone, backed by a full range of sound effects.

Joe and Me at the Play

Unfortunately we have no details about the origins of this
piece. We would be grateful for any information.

Giving Notes

This sketch was originally performed by Julie Walters in
Victoria Wood, As Seen on TV. It is a good example of the
modern revue style of which Victoria Wood is a leading
exponent, chiefly on television but also in a series of sell-
out solo tours.

Moody Dane

Herbert Farjeon was the major revue librettist of the 1930s,
and his knowledge of Shakespeare, as a theatre critic and
author, perhaps accounts for the series of four *Theme
Songs for Shakespeare* (including *Moody Dane*) which
appeared in *Nine Sharp* at the Little Theatre. The various
characters are portrayed as heroes of the silver screen, this
particular number being subtitled 'For a Hollywood
Hamlet'. With his sister Eleanor, Herbert Farjeon also
wrote a number of musical plays around this time, such
as *The Two Bouquets* (1936) and *An Elephant in Arcady*
(1938). Soon after the Shakespeare Memorial Theatre was
built in 1932, Farjeon wrote that Stratford was 'the one
spot on the map where you can produce Shakespeare
as badly, or as well, as you like and be sure of making
a good profit', an idea which the current Board of
Governors might question.

Rehearsing Hamlet

Peter Hall's production of *Hamlet* starred Albert Finney.

It completed the National Theatre's tenure of the Old Vic and opened the new Lyttelton Theatre in March 1976.

Ian Charleson Plays Hamlet

Charleson took over from Daniel Day-Lewis in Richard Eyre's production. When ill-health forced him to withdraw from the cast he was replaced by his understudy, Jeremy Northam (later an acclaimed Berowne for the RSC). Charleson's many appearances at the RNT included Sky Masterson in *Guys and Dolls*, also directed by Eyre. Prior to this he had played modern and classical roles with the RSC, including an exquisitely-sung Ariel (music by Guy Woolfenden) to Michael Hordern's Prospero.

Fear No More

Sondheim wrote this setting of lines from *Cymbeline*
for Burt Shevelove's adaptation of Aristophanes' comedy
The Frogs. The musical features a contest between
Shakespeare and Shaw, who attempt to outdo each other
with quotations from their work. On the topic of 'life and
death', Shaw's extract from *Saint Joan* is countered by
this version of *Fear No More*. The first production of *The
Frogs* was mounted in the Yale University swimming pool
with an aquatic chorus which included Meryl Streep and
Sigourney Weaver.

Part Two

A Warwickshire Lad

Dibdin's air was composed for Garrick's Shakespeare Jubilee of 1769. Despite the fact that it did not mark any particular anniversary and that not one word of Shakespeare
was spoken all weekend, the event was the first major
Stratford celebration and can be seen as the genesis of the
Shakespeare Industry. Dibdin, an actor, singer, composer,
playwright and manager, performed prototype one-man
revues at his own theatre in the Strand, where he com-
bined songs, monologues and topical sketches. In our
production this was a company number; the reprise was
sung under an umbrella and sou'westers, in keeping with
the waterlogged conditions of the song's première.

Birthday Celebrations

The Tercentenary of Shakespeare's birth in 1864 provided
the impetus which led directly to the building of the first
Stratford theatre in 1879, after fifteen years of fund-raising.
Since the beginning of this century, Shakespeare's birthday
has been celebrated annually in Stratford by a weekend
of civic events. Those who have attended the birthday
lunch in large (often windswept) marquees in the Bancroft
Gardens, may well think that little has changed when
they read Mr Creswick's speech from 1864.

So That's The Way You Like It

Beyond the Fringe was mounted as a late-night revue for the Edinburgh Festival in 1960. It brought together talent from Oxford and Cambridge, and transferred to the West End (where it ran for five years) and Broadway. Peter Cook was already established in London as the principal author of the revue *Pieces of Eight* (1959), starring Kenneth Williams. Michael Frayn recalls Alan Bennett telling him that 'they had conceived *Beyond the Fringe* simply by standing round and deciding what they loathed, then sending it up. It sounds almost too admirably rational to be true.' The success of the revue was partly responsible for the craze for satire in the sixties, although this manifested itself more on television than in the theatre, with programmes such as *That Was The Week That Was* and *Not So Much a Programme, More a Way of Life*.

Ladies of London

Ned Sherrin, the doyen of television satire (including *TW3*), directed one of the most successful revues of the seventies in both London and New York – *Side by Side by Sondheim*. He collaborated with Caryl Brahms on a number of musical entertainments, notably *Beecham, Sing a Rude Song* and *The Mitford Girls*. The adaptation of Caryl Brahms and S.J.Simon's comic novel *No Bed For Bacon* has had two scores – the 1959 original by Malcolm Williamson and another by Tom Gregory and John Scott for a revival in 1963. When Ned Sherrin sent us these lyrics he was unable to find either version, hence this new setting for the four ladies of the night, played by both the male and female members of the company.

The Repertory Actor

Guy Boas was a regular contributor to *Punch* in the twenties and thirties, particularly of comic theatrical verse. In his other life he was Headmaster of a boys' preparatory school in Chelsea, where he enthusiastically produced the annual school play. We have rewritten the last stanza of this poem, which now deals with Romeo rather than Juliet, and thus introduces the next item.

Wherefore Art Thou Juliet?

This is the sketch that has been suggested to us most frequently, but nobody seemed quite sure of its provenance. When we finally settled the matter, the Lord Chamberlain's Collection at the British Library proved inaccessible: the text was locked away in a warehouse in deepest Essex which was undergoing a long asbestos-removal programme. Eventually we transcribed the material from a rare Alan Melville LP. It was originally performed by Thelma Ruby and Hugh Paddick under the title *Yonder Blessed Moon*, and it seems that the present title was introduced during the pre-London tour.

Cravin' for the Avon

The 1956 musical *Grab Me A Gondola* had a long London run starring Denis Quilley and Joan Heal – both veterans of revues at the Lyric, the Globe and the Royal Court. Our solo singer vamped her way through the list of desirable Shakespeare heroes backed by a 1950s boy/girl chorus clustered around a period microphone.

William and the Lost Tourist

Richmal Crompton frequently refers to Shakespeare in the *Just William* books, and it was difficult to select just one extract. However, this splendid satire on tourism, whilst not obvious revue material, does play particularly well. The prose divides up neatly between a narrator, William, Miss Burford and Mrs Maloney.

Teach Me, Dear Creature

Julian Slade has composed settings for many Shakespeare songs and his version of *The Comedy of Errors*, composed in the same year as *Salad Days,* was the first musical written specially for television. It starred Joan Plowright and Patricia Routledge, later emerging in a stage version at the Bristol Old Vic.

Seeing Stratford

Published in the 1920s, this essay, describing a first visit to Stratford, was reprinted in 1981 with a postscript. By this time, the author had lived in Alveston, a mile or so from Shakespeare's Birthplace, for twenty-five years. This extract was spoken over a musical interlude between the two verses of the previous number.

Theatre Visitors

An excerpt from Susan Hill's evocation of Stratford and its environs, this piece deals with the time before she 'married into Shakespeare', as she puts it. Her husband is Professor Stanley Wells, Editor of the Oxford Shakespeare, Director of the Shakespeare Institute and Vice-Chairman of the RSC.

The Forest of Arden

Maureen Lipman's Stratford career was all too brief,

although she did play the Princess of France in the BBC Television production of *Love's Labour's Lost*. Her one-woman revue *Re: Joyce*, celebrating the life and work of Joyce Grenfell (who frustratingly seems not to have touched upon Shakespeare in her writing) has been successfully revived for several London seasons.

Anectdotage

These theatre stories, retold by Derek Nimmo in his book *As the Actress Said to the Bishop*, were read by the whole company, the apocryphal Donald Wolfit tale leading naturally to . . .

The Night I Appeared as Macbeth

William Hargreaves' song parodies the time-honoured practice of 'improving' on the Bard (cf. Nahum Tate's *King Lear* and *The Music Hall Shakespeare*). In a third verse (which we have had to cut for reasons of length) Hargreaves' Macbeth complains:

The play tho' ascribed to Bill Shakespeare,
To me lacked both polish and tone,
So I put bits in from Miss Elinor Glyn,
Nat Gould, and some bits of my own.

The Verse Problem

Yet more fascinating insights from *Shakespeare: the Truth*.

Exam Questions

A snippet from Richard Armour's wry response to the Bard. Armour, an American academic, hoped this popular book would 'contribute to a clearer misunderstanding' of Shakespeare. The characters of Henry V, Juliet and Hamlet are established and proceed to sing . . .

Give Us A Rest

Written for a late-night revue at the 1953 Edinburgh Festival, *Give Us A Rest* surprisingly did not survive the transfer to London. In the intervening forty-one years, Sandy Wilson had mislaid the last verse and so has kindly supplied a replacement for us.

The Curtain

See *The Repertory Actor*.

Brush Up Your Shakespeare (reprise)

See earlier note. The classroom howlers are genuine.

Curtain Speech

An extract from Ronald Harwood's West End success which starred Freddie Jones as 'Sir' (loosely based on Sir Donald Wolfit) and Tom Courtenay as the eponymous dresser Norman. The play, set in a wartime provincial theatre, was later filmed, starring Courtenay and Albert Finney.

That Shakespearian Rag

We first came across this song as a reference in T.S. Eliot's *The Waste Land*: 'O O O O that Shakespeherian Rag – / It's so elegant / So intelligent'. Songs like Irving Berlin's *Alexander's Rag-time Band* (1911) changed the face of popular music, and *That Shakespearian Rag* was another example of a craze that coincided with the advent of modern spectacular revue. Shows of the period sometimes took their titles from the rag-time songs they featured, *Everybody's Doing It* being a prime example.

Let's Do It

The lyrics for this song have often been altered. Noël Coward wrote new couplets to fit the Cole Porter melody for many different occasions (first recording it in 1934), and we followed his lead, concocting our version for a charity gala at Stratford in 1991. The number seemed a perfect finale to the revue, and we would encourage future casts to slot in topical references of their own. We are slightly ashamed to admit that we used this item as a planned encore, completing the revue proper with the previous item. Coward boasted that he had seen every revue worth mentioning in London, Paris and New York from *Hullo Rag-time!* in 1912 to *Oh! Calcutta!* in 1970. Of his own work in the field, *This Year of Grace* (1928) was, he ventured to suggest, 'the most perfect, the wittiest, the most beautiful, glamorous, funniest revue ever produced'.

Ackowledgements

We are grateful to the following publishers, copyright holders and agents for permission to reproduce material in *The Shakespeare Revue*. Every effort has been made to trace the copyright holders. If omissions have accidentally occurred, please contact the publisher and they will be included in any future edition.

Bernard Levin for the extract from *Enthusiasms*; Chappells for *Brush Up Your Shakespeare* from *Kiss Me Kate* by Cole Porter; Methuen for the two extracts from *Shakespeare: the Truth* by Patrick Barlow; Doreen Harris for *Othello* by Leon Cortez; Jack Klaff for *I'm in the RSC!*; Chappells for *Witches' Brew* from *Hallelujah Baby!* by Jule Styne, Betty Comden and Adolph Green; the Estates of Alan Melville and Charles Zwar for *Which Witch?*; Roger Pringle for the extract from *Portrait of a Stratford Year*; Stephen Fry and Hugh Laurie for *Shakespeare Masterclass*; Michael Green and Sheil Land Associates for the extract from the Revised Edition of *The Art of Coarse Acting* © Michael Green 1964, 1980, 1994, published by Samuel French; Tim Brooke-Taylor and Bill Oddie for *Swap a Jest*; Frank Muir and Denis Norden for the extract from *Take It From Here*; Methuen for *Giving Notes* from *Up To You, Porky* by Victoria Wood; the Estates of Herbert Farjeon and John Pritchett for *Moody Dane*; Michael Joseph Ltd. for the extract from *Peter Hall's Diaries*; Richard Eyre and Bloomsbury Publishing for the extract from *Utopia and Other Places*; Warner Chappells for *Fear No More* by Stephen Sondheim; Alan Bennett, Peter Cook, Jonathan Miller and Dudley Moore for *So That's the Way You Like It* from *Beyond the Fringe*; Ned Sherrin for *Ladies of London*; Express Newspapers and The Punch Library for *The Repertory Actor* and *The Curtain* by Guy Boas; the Estate of Alan Melville for *Wherefore Art Thou Juliet?*; Chappells for *Cravin' for the Avon* from *Grab me a Gondola* by James Gilbert and Julian More; Macmillan Childrens' Books for *William and the Lost Tourist* by Richmal Crompton; Julian Slade for *Teach Me, Dear Creature*; Methuen for the extract from *Apes and Angels* © the Estate of J.B. Priestley, reprinted by kind permission of Peters Fraser and Dunlop Group Ltd.; Michael Joseph Ltd. for the extract from *Shakespeare Country* by Susan Hill; Maureen Lipman and Robson Books for the extract from *How Was It For You?*; Derek Nimmo and Robson Books for the extracts from *As the Actress Said to the Bishop*; McGraw-Hill Book Co.Inc for the extract from *Twisted Tales from Shakespeare* by Richard Armour; Amber Lane Press for the extract from *The Dresser* by Ronald Harwood; lyric reproduction of *That Shakespearian Rag* by Gene Buck, Herman Ruby and David Stamper by kind permission of Carlin Music Corp. UK Administrator; Chappells and the Noël Coward Estate for *Let's Do It* by Cole Porter and Noël Coward.

Illustrations

We would like to thank the various artists for their generosity in providing illustrations. Larry, Chris Mould, Lesley Saddington and Sandy Wilson kindly gave us original work. The following allowed us to use existing material: Deirdre Clancy, Nicholas Garland, Gary, William Hewison, Gerald Scarfe, Antony Sher, Ralph Steadman, Mark Thompson, Sylvestra le Touzel and Anthony Ward. The cartoons by Mel Calman and ffolkes appear by permission of Claire and Stephanie Calman and the Punch Library respectively, and the drawing by Arthur Keene by permission of Roger Pringle.

Index